BEHIND THE PLATE

NATIONAL LEAGUE CENTRAL

THE CHICAGO CUBS, THE CINCINNATI REDS, THE HOUSTON ASTROS, THE MILWAUKEE BREWERS, THE PITTSBURGH PIRATES, AND THE ST. LOUIS CARDINALS

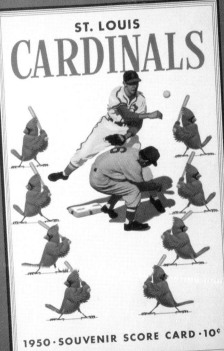

ST. LOUIS

CARDINALS

1950·SOUVENIR SCORE CARD·10¢

BY JOHN SILBAUGH

The Child's World

National League Central: The Chicago Cubs, the Cincinnati Reds, the Houston Astros, the Milwaukee Brewers, the Pittsburgh Pirates, and the St. Louis Cardinals
Published in the United States of America by The Child's World®
PO Box 326 • Chanhassen, MN 55317-0326 • 800-599-READ • www.childsworld.com

Acknowledgements:
The Child's World®: Mary Berendes, Publishing Director

Editorial Directions, Inc.: E. Russell Primm, Editorial Director; Matthew Messbarger, Line Editor; Katie Marsico, Assistant Editor; Susan Hindman, Copy Editor; Sarah E. De Capua, Proofreader; Kevin Cunningham, Fact Checker; Tim Griffin/IndexServ, Indexer; James Buckley Jr., Photo Researcher and Selector

The Design Lab: Kathleen Petelinsek, Art Direction and Design; Kari Thornborough, Page Production

Cover:
Mark Prior

Page one:
St. Louis
Cardinals
souvenir
score card

Photos:
AP: 13, 16
Bettmann/Corbis: 7, 14, 20, 31
Gary Brady/Reuters/Corbis: 38
Gary Caskey/Reuters/Corbis: 17
Alan Diaz/AP: 24
Stephen Dunn /Allsport/Getty: 28
Jonathan Ernst/Reuters/Corbis: 10
Tom Gannam/AP: 41
Morry Gash/AP: 29
Dan Helms/NewSport/Corbis: 18
Brad Mangin/MLB/Getty: 35
Sue Ogrocki/Reuters/Corbis: 9
Rich Pilling/MLB/Getty: 26, 33
Rucker Archive: 4, 6
Transcendental Graphics: 1
Dilip Vishwanat/Getty: 37
David Zalubowski/AP: 23
John Zich/NewSport/Corbis: Cover

Library of Congress Cataloging-in-Publication Data
Silbaugh, John.
  National League Central / by John Silbaugh.
    p. cm. — (Behind the plate)
  Includes index.
  ISBN 1-59296-361-7 (library bound : alk. paper) 1. National League of Professional Baseball Clubs—History—Juvenile literature. 2. Baseball teams—United States—Juvenile literature. I. Title. II. Series.
  GV875.A3S55 2004
  796.357'64'0973—dc22   2004016847

Table of Contents

Team: Chicago Cubs

Founded: 1874

Park: Wrigley Field

Park Opened: 1914

Colors: Blue and red

Team: Cincinnati Reds

Founded: 1869

Park: Great American Ballpark

Park Opened: 2003

Colors: Red and black

Team: Houston Astros

Founded: 1962

Park: Minute Maid Park

Park Opened: 2000

Colors: Navy blue, burnt orange, and pale yellow

M aybe there really is something to curses. Here's how the story goes: The Chicago Cubs were in the **World Series** in 1945. As a publicity stunt, a local business owner tried to bring a goat into Wrigley Field for one of the games against the Detroit Tigers. The ticket takers, of course, would not allow it. So the man put a curse on the Cubs, vowing they would never again win the World Series. And you know what? They haven't.

The other teams in the National League (NL) Central, the division in which the Cubs play, must wonder if the curse is contagious. Ever since the current NL Central first took shape in 1994, none of the teams has won a World Series. What's more, none has even made it to the World Series until St. Louis in 2004.

CHICAGO BASE BALL CLUB OF 1908.
WORLD'S CHAMPIONS.

1—Slagle
2—Reulbach
3—Evers
4—Schulte
5—Moran
6—Kling
7—Overall
8—Hofman
9—Fraser
10—Tinker
11—Lundgren
12—Sheckard
13—Steinfeldt
14—Howard
15—Pfeister
16—Brown
17—Chance
18—Durbin

1908 Cubs

Before 1994, there was no Central Division. The NL's 14 teams were divided into two divisions of seven teams each, the East and the West. When the major leagues realigned for the 1994 season and added an extra tier of playoffs to include a **wild-card** team, the five-member Central was born. The Chicago Cubs, Pittsburgh Pirates, and St. Louis Cardinals were taken from the East; the Cincinnati Reds and the Houston Astros were lifted from the West.

In 1998, baseball expanded with the addition of the American League's (AL's) Tampa Bay Devil Rays and the NL's Arizona Diamondbacks. But that meant there were 15 teams in each league. An odd number wouldn't work, or else every day there would be one team that couldn't play. To get each league to an even number, the AL's Milwaukee Brewers shifted to the NL Central. Since then, the division has remained the same.

Though the NL Central has yet to produce a World Series champion, the division does not lack **tradition**—far from it. The six division franchises, in fact, have produced some of baseball's greatest teams and some of its greatest individuals. Want to know what we mean? Then read on, and you'll find out lots more about the NL Central.

Team: Milwaukee Brewers
Founded: 1969
Park: Miller Park
Park Opened: 2001
Colors: Midnight blue and gold

Team: Pittsburgh Pirates
Founded: 1882
Park: PNC Park
Park Opened: 2001
Colors: Black and gold

Team: St. Louis Cardinals
Founded: 1876
Park: Busch Stadium
Park Opened: 1966
Colors: Cardinal red and navy blue

CHAPTER ONE

The Chicago Cubs

The Chicago Cubs, one of the original members of the NL, are a team rich in tradition. Unfortunately for Cubs fans, though, the tradition has not usually been a winning one. When the team has managed to reach the **postseason,** only heartbreak has followed.

The 2003 Cubs won a thrilling NL Central chase before beating the Atlanta Braves in the Division Series for their first postseason win in 58 years. Then, after building a three-games-to-one lead against Florida in the NL Championship Series (NLCS), they took a 3–0 lead into the eighth inning of Game 6 at home. But they let the game and, eventually, the NL **pennant** slip away.

The Cubs' last World Series win came in 1908. They last

CUBS

Mordeon Brown
OF THE
CHICAGO NATIONALS

Mordecai Brown

Infielder Ernie Banks was so popular that he
is still affectionately known as "Mr. Cub."

appeared in the series in 1945. The good news is that
if ever a team was due, it's the Cubs.

When most people think of the Cubs, they think
of Wrigley Field. Tucked into Wrigleyville, one of
Chicago's North Side neighborhoods, the oldest
ballpark in the NL is an institution. The Cubs—and
their opponents—have been hammering baseballs off

Mordecai Brown
was called "Three
Finger" because a
boyhood farming
accident took two
fingers on his right
(pitching) hand.

The Cubs teams

of the early 1900s

featured the

famous double-play

combination of

Tinker-to-Evers-to-

Chance. Shortstop

Joe Tinker, second

baseman Johnny

Evers, and first

baseman and

Manager Frank

Chance erased

many opposition

base runners.

Wrigley's brick walls (and over them onto Waveland and Sheffield avenues) since 1916.

The Cubs have not always been the Cubs. They played in the National Association in 1874 and 1875 as the Chicago White Stockings. After becoming a charter member of the NL in 1876, they had at least 16 different nicknames, including the Orphans, the Colts, and the Remnants. In 1902, the club underwent a major rebuilding: As many as 20 rookies were on the roster. A local sportswriter dubbed the young squad "the Cubs." The name stuck and was officially adopted five years later.

The Cubs became a powerhouse soon after the turn of the century. In 1906, they set major league records with 116 wins and a .763 winning percentage. But they were upset in the World Series that year by the crosstown White Sox. The Cubs returned to beat the Detroit Tigers for the crown in 1907 and 1908. They were the first back-to-back World Series champions in baseball history.

The pitching star of that early Cubs **dynasty** was Mordecai "Three Finger" Brown. He won 20 games or more in six straight seasons and added four World Series wins from 1906 to 1908.

Sammy Sosa is one of baseball's most spectacular sluggers.

From 1982 to 1998, broadcaster Harry Caray was a Cubs institution. Harry led Cubs fans in the traditional seventh-inning stretch song, "Take Me Out to the Ball Game." His cries of "Cubs Win! Cubs Win!" after a Chicago victory became well known.

The current Cubs feature a squad of excellent young pitchers such as Kerry Wood.

Cubs teams since then have often been bad, occasionally good (NL pennants in 1929, 1932, 1935, 1938, and 1945), but never quite good enough. Chicago has had some tremendous individual talent, however. In 1930, Hack Wilson set the major league record with 191 runs batted in (RBIs) to go along with 56 homers (an NL record for 68 years). In 1958, shortstop Ernie Banks became the first player to win a Most Valuable Player (MVP) award while playing for a losing team. "Mr. Cub" won the award again the next year to become the first back-to-back MVP in the NL. Though winning was a rare event for his Cubs, Ernie was always enthusiastic. He was famous for saying, "What a great day for baseball, let's play two!"

Today, no one defines the Cubs more than Sammy Sosa. Once a skinny, speedy outfielder with a bit of power, Sosa became one of the greatest home run hitters the game has ever seen. In 1998, he was in a home run duel with the Cardinals' Mark McGwire. Each slugger wanted to break Roger Maris's major league record of 61 homers. And both did, though McGwire's 70 topped Sosa's 66. The next year, McGwire hit 65 and Sosa 63. Two years later, Sosa and the Giants' Barry Bonds went after McGwire's mark. Bonds set a new record with 73, while Sosa hit 64 home runs. Sammy is the only player to top 60 homers in three different seasons, yet he didn't win the home run title in any of the three! These days, a pitching staff that includes the powerful young arms of Kerry Wood and Mark Prior fits nicely with Sosa. Cubs fans have renewed hope that their year is coming . . . soon!

Wrigley Field did not have lights until 1988. While night baseball was introduced in the 1930s, Cubs fans saw day games at Wrigley for 72 years. Finally, on August 8, 1988, the lights came on at Wrigley as the Cubs hosted the Phillies. As luck would have it, the game was rained out in the fourth inning. Fans waited another 24 hours for the first official night game, which the Cubs won, 6–4, over the Mets.

CHAPTER TWO

The Cincinnati Reds

The Cincinnati Reds—originally called the Red Stockings—were baseball's first all-**professional** team. They have played NL baseball nearly continuously since 1876. After being kicked out of the NL in 1880, the Reds helped found the rival American Association in 1882. They came back to the Senior Circuit, a nickname for the NL due to it being the older of the two major leagues, in 1890. For almost three decades, though, the Reds were one of the NL's least successful teams, never finishing higher than third.

All that changed in 1919. Future Hall of Famer Edd Roush and Heinie Groh led the Reds to 96 wins and the team's first pennant. Still, they were a heavy **underdog** team to the AL champion White Sox. Cincinnati won anyway, five games to three. Afterward, eight White Sox players, including "Shoeless" Joe Jackson, admitted to taking bribes to lose the World

Frank Robinson's MVP season helped carry the Reds to the pennant in 1961.

Series on purpose. They were banned for life from baseball.

After a 20-year drought, the Reds won consecutive pennants in 1939 and 1940. They lost to Joe DiMaggio's Yankees in '39, but rebounded to beat the Tigers in seven games in '40. It would be the last Cincinnati championship for 35 years.

In the meantime, a pair of sluggers entertained Reds fans: Ted Kluszewski and Frank Robinson. Kluszewski, a first baseman, hit 251 homers for the Reds from 1948 to 1957. "Klu" was well known

In 1944, pitcher Joe Nuxhall became the youngest player ever to appear in a big-league game. He was just 15 and a student in high school when he made his debut for the Reds that year.

Pitcher Tom Browning pitched the only perfect game in Reds history on September 16, 1988, against the Dodgers.

for cutting the sleeves of his jersey to show off his massive muscles. Robinson, one of the first African Americans to play for the Reds, hit 38 homers in his debut in 1956 to win Rookie of the Year honors. In 1961, the superstar outfielder led the Reds to a pennant, hitting .323 with 37 homers and 124 RBIs.

This base hit was the 4,192nd of Pete Rose's career, breaking Ty Cobb's all-time record.

He was the NL MVP. In 1965, though, the Reds traded Robinson to Baltimore, where a year later, he led the way to the **Triple Crown** and a World Series win for the Orioles.

In 1970, the Reds moved into Riverfront Stadium. There, the Reds built a dynasty, winning six division titles, four pennants, and two World Series championships in the '70s. Managed for most of the 1970s by George "Sparky" Anderson, the "Big Red Machine" had All-Stars (and future Hall of Famers) up and down the lineup.

In 1975, the Reds won a team-record 108 games. Then came a classic seven-game World Series win over the Boston Red Sox that is regarded by many as the greatest series ever. Joe Morgan, the NL MVP, delivered the winning hit in the ninth inning of Game 7.

The team was perhaps even more dominant the next year. After winning 102 regular-season games, the Reds swept through the postseason without a loss to claim back-to-back World Series crowns. Morgan was the NL MVP again that year. Pitcher Pat Zachary was Rookie of the Year. Rawly Eastwick was the top relief pitcher. Four players won Gold Glove Awards. It was truly one of the best teams of all time.

Catcher Ernie Lombardi, pitcher Bucky Walters, and first baseman Frank McCormick won back-to-back-to-back NL MVP awards from 1938 to 1940. This made the Reds the first team to have three different players win the award in consecutive seasons.

Powel Crosley bought the Reds in 1934 and changed the name of their home from Redland Field to Crosley Field. The next year, Crosley got permission from Major League Baseball's commissioner to put lights in his ballpark. On May 24, 1935, the Reds beat the Phillies 2–1 in the first night game in major league baseball history.

Pete Rose left the team as a **free agent** after the '78 season. In 1984, he was re-signed as a player and manager for the team. On September 11, 1985, he broke Ty Cobb's major league record with his 4,192nd career hit. As a manager, Rose nurtured a young team of future stars including Barry Larkin, Paul O'Neill, and Eric Davis. Rose left the Reds in '89 after he was banned from baseball for betting on games.

Johnny Bench combined hitting and defense like no other catcher before him.

Ken Griffey Jr. followed in his dad's footsteps in Cincinnati.

Under Manager Lou Piniella, the Reds returned to the World Series in 1990. After edging the Pirates in the NLCS, the Reds swept the favored A's in one of the greatest World Series upsets ever.

In 1995, Cincinnati won the first-ever NL Central Division crown. Larkin, a shortstop, was named the NL MVP after hitting .319 with 51 stolen bases. Then in 2000, Reds fans welcomed home Ken Griffey Jr. The former Mariners star had played

In 1938, Reds pitcher Johnny Vander Meer made history by throwing two no-hitters in a row. On June 11, Vander Meer no-hit the Boston Braves. Four days later, in the first night game played at Brooklyn's Ebbets Field, Vander Meer held the Dodgers without a hit.

17

In 1869, club
president Aaron
Champion decided
to sign all nine of
his Red Stockings
players to full-season
contracts. The
total payroll was
about $11,000, with
shortstop George
Wright the highest
paid at almost $2,000.

Reds catcher
Johnny Bench (1970,
1972), outfielder
Peter Rose (1973),
second baseman
Joe Morgan (1975,
1976), and outfielder
George Foster (1977)
combined to win six
NL MVP awards in
the 1970s.

as a young boy on the Riverfront turf during his
father's days with the Big Red Machine. At the same
time he returned, plans were made to build the Reds
a new home. The Great American Ball Park opened
on March 31, 2003.

Adam Dunn is a powerful home run threat for the current Reds.

CHAPTER THREE

The Houston Astros

The Houston Astros have been the NL Central's most successful team, finishing first or second in 10 of the division's first 11 seasons. Baseball in Houston hasn't always been this good, however. Houston joined the NL in 1962 as the Colt .45s. The team's first home was the 33,000-seat Colt Stadium. Noted for high heat, humidity, and big, hungry mosquitoes, Colt Stadium wasn't the best place to watch baseball. The team wasn't much better, losing 96 games in each of its three years there.

In 1965, the Colts took their game indoors to the new Houston Astrodome and became the Astros. The world's first multipurpose, domed stadium was named to honor Houston's importance to the space program and was known as The Eighth Wonder of the World.

The Astros managed their first winning season in 1972, finishing second in the NL West with 84 wins. Under Manager Bill Virdon, the Astros

Nolan Ryan is major league baseball's all-time strikeout king.

improved steadily through the late'70s, finally winning the NL West in 1980 in a one-game playoff over the Dodgers. Great pitching proved to be the Astros' ticket to the playoffs. Strikeout king Nolan Ryan joined a pitching squad already stocked with Joe Niekro, J. R. Richard, Ken Forsch, and Vern Ruhle. In the first of many playoff disappointments for Houston, the Astros lost a thrilling NLCS to the Phillies, three games to two. Four of the five contests were decided in extra innings.

The Astros returned to the postseason the next year as division winners in the second half of the strike-interrupted season. Ryan led the league with a 1.69 earned run average (ERA) and pitched his record fifth no-hitter. Cold bats again dashed the team's World Series hopes, however, in a division-series loss to the Dodgers.

Rookie manager Hal Lanier steered the Astros to another division crown in 1986. Pitcher Mike Scott led the majors in strikeouts and ERAs, winning the **Cy Young Award.** First baseman Glenn Davis paced the team with 31 homers, the most for an Astros player in 17 seasons. Scott continued his brilliance in the NLCS against the Mets, winning twice while striking out 19 and yielding only eight hits and one run. Still, New York won a 16-inning thriller in Game 6 to take the series.

Three straight second-place finishes from 1994 to 1996 left the team hungry for the top spot in the NL Central. In 1997, under rookie manager (and former Houston pitcher) Larry Dierker, the Astros reached that peak. Despite a modest 84–78 record, Houston had its first division title since 1986. However, the Atlanta Braves quickly knocked the Astros out of the playoffs in a three-game division-series sweep.

A huge eight-player trade with the Reds during the 1971 winter meetings brought first baseman Lee May, among others, to Houston. The trade would prove to be costly, however, as future Hall of Famer Joe Morgan and outfielder Cesar Geronimo would become important parts in Cincinnati's Big Red Machine.

Outfielder Jose Cruz ranks in the Astros' all-time top 10 in every major batting category. From 1975 to 1987, he compiled a .292 batting average, with 335 doubles, 80 triples, 138 homers, 942 RBIs, and 288 stolen bases. Cruz led the team in hitting six seasons and was the team's RBI leader seven times.

The Astros clinched the 1986 West Division title when Mike Scott pitched a no-hitter to beat the Giants 2–0.

In 1998, the Astros fielded their best team, which won a club-record 102 games to easily claim its second straight division title. A potent offense featured second baseman Craig Biggio, left fielder Moises Alou, and first baseman Jeff Bagwell. Pitcher Randy Johnson was 10–1 with a 1.28 ERA after coming to Houston in a midseason trade. In perhaps their most bitter playoff failure, however, the Astros lost to the Padres.

A record 2.7 million fans came to the Astrodome in 1999 to mark its 35th and final season. The team said good-bye with another banner year, winning 97 games and a third straight division title. Bagwell had a huge year, with 42 home runs and 126 RBIs. He finished second in NL MVP voting to Chipper Jones of the Braves, who also beat the Astros in the division series.

In 2000, the Astros moved into Enron Field— their new real-grass ballpark with a retractable roof (meaning it could be mechanically pulled back to open the stadium to the sky). More than 3 million fans came to see a higher-scoring brand of baseball. The Astros set franchise records with 249 home

First baseman Jeff Bagwell has been a consistent force for more than a decade.

Second baseman Craig Biggio and first baseman Jeff Bagwell have been Astros stars since 1988 and 1991, respectively. At various times over the years, Lance Berkman, Sean Berry, Derek Bell, and Geoff Blum have joined the pair in a "Killer B's" lineup.

Roy Oswalt won 19 games in just his second big-league season in 2002.

runs and 938 runs in 2000. A division championship in 2001, followed by a three-game sweep by the Braves in the divisional playoffs, left the team zero-for-seven in postseason play. The Astros' new home was renamed Minute Maid Park in 2002. In 2004, Houston earned a wild-card berth and won its first playoff series, beating Atlanta in the opening round. Only a seven-game loss to St. Louis in the NLCS kept the Astros from the World Series.

CHAPTER FOUR

The Milwaukee Brewers

The Brewers are the NL Central's newest team, having relocated to the Senior Circuit after the 1997 season.

To illustrate the full story of major league baseball in Milwaukee, a moving van would come in handy. Today's Brewers are the third different club based in Milwaukee, and all three have changed addresses at least once. These Brewers began farther west as the Seattle Pilots in 1969. After one year, they came to Milwaukee and were renamed the Brewers.

It took the franchise nine years to post a winning record. One highlight from this period was the arrival in 1974 of 18-year-old shortstop Robin Yount. The future Hall of Famer went on to play his entire career with the Brewers. He retired in 1993 as the team's career leader in almost every batting category, including hits (3,142).

Beginning in 1978, the club ran off a streak of six straight winning seasons and 11 out of 15 years

at .500 or better. The Brewers of this era were a feared team of home run hitters. Yount, first baseman Cecil Cooper and outfielders Ben Oglivie and Gorman Thomas powered a team that topped the major leagues in 1980 in homers, total bases, and slugging percentage. Third baseman Paul Molitor got on base for the big bashers.

After trades brought pitching help in starter Pete Vuckovich and reliever Rollie Fingers, the Brewers won a split-season championship in the 1981 strike-shortened year. Fingers was brilliant, going 6–3 with a 1.04 ERA and 28 **saves.** After the season, he became the first relief pitcher in history to win both Cy Young and MVP honors. The Brewers' spectacular season ended in a tightly contested division series loss to the Yankees.

With Yount, Vuckovich, and Fingers again leading the way, the Brewers won 95 games in 1982. After the team got off to a slow start, Manager Buck Rodgers was replaced by hitting coach Harvey Kuenn. "Harvey's Wallbangers" went 72–43 in the season's last four months to capture the AL East crown by a game over the Orioles. With Vuckovich

Robin Yount won MVP awards while playing two of the most demanding positions in baseball: shortstop and center field.

On April 14, 1993, the Brewers' lineup included pitcher Graeme Lloyd and catcher David Nilsson. It was the first all-Australian pitcher/catcher combination in major league history.

From 1970 to 1998, the Brewers were run by Allan "Bud" Selig, who then became commissioner of Major League Baseball. His daughter Wendy Selig-Prieb is currently the Brewers' chairwoman of the board.

Paul Molitor hit .302 for Milwaukee's AL champs in 1982.

Robin Yount was

the AL MVP as a

shortstop in 1982.

He was the MVP

as a center fielder

in 1989.

winning the Cy Young Award and Yount (.331 average, 29 homers, 114 RBIs) the MVP, the Brewers became the only AL team to win both major awards in consecutive seasons.

After falling behind the Angels two games to none in the NLCS that year, the Brewers swept the next three games to earn their first trip to the World Series. Against the Cardinals, the Brewers took a three-games-to-two lead to St. Louis's Busch Stadium. But their future division rivals won the last two games to capture the series.

The 1987 Brewers jumped out of the gate with 13 straight wins on their way to a 91-win season. Unfortunately, the team also lost 12 in a row in May to fall out of first place.

After winning 92 games under Manager Phil Garner in 1992, the Brewers began a streak of losing seasons—12 straight through 2004. A seven-player trade in 2000 brought slugging first baseman Richie Sexson. The next year, Sexson's eighth-inning homer helped the Brewers open their new home, Miller Park, with a 5–4 win over the Reds.

Brewers pitcher Ben Sheets struck out a club-record 18 batters while beating Atlanta 4–1 in a game in May of 2004.

One of the Brewers' current stars is speedy outfielder Scott Podsednik.

CHAPTER FIVE

The Pittsburgh Pirates

With a history dating back to the 1880s, the Pittsburgh Pirates are one of the more senior teams in the Senior Circuit. They were originally named the Alleghenys after one of two rivers (the other being the Monongahela) that merge in the Steel City to form the Ohio River. They got their current name after the team lured second baseman Louis Bierbauer away from the Philadelphia Athletics of the rival American Association. The A's cried foul, accusing the cross-state team of "pirating" their team. Pittsburgh kept the player and got a new nickname, too.

In the early 1900s, the Pirates were the NL's dominant team, winning championships in the first three seasons of the new century. After the 1903 season, the Pirates played the AL's Boston Pilgrims (known later as the Red Sox) in the first World Series. Boston won it, five games to three. Two standouts were Pirates shortstop Honus Wagner and Boston pitcher Cy Young. Wagner would go on to become

Ralph Kiner swung a big bat for the Pirates in the late 1940s and early 1950s.

part of the first class of inductees into baseball's Hall of Fame, while Young was in the second class. In 1909, the Pirates again reached the World Series, edging the Detroit Tigers four games to three.

Led by Max Carey, Kiki Cuyler, and Pie Traynor (all future Hall of Famers), the Pirates returned to the World Series in 1925. Down three games to one, Pittsburgh rallied to defeat the Washington Senators and their **ace,** Walter "Big Train" Johnson. A strong Pirates team became even stronger with the addition of the Waner brothers (Lloyd "Little Poison" and Paul "Big Poison"). They took the NL crown again

Dick Stuart, the first baseman on the 1960 World Series championship team, was such a poor fielder that he earned the nickname "Dr. Strangeglove," after a movie of that era called *Dr. Strangelove.*

The Pirates made history on September 1, 1971, when they fielded what is believed to be the first all-minority starting lineup in major league baseball.

two years later, only to have the misfortune of facing maybe the best team in baseball history. The fabled '27 Yankees, with their "Murderers Row" lineup featuring Babe Ruth and Lou Gehrig, swept the series in four straight games.

For most of the next three decades, Pirates history featured little success. There were several outstanding individual achievements, however. Slugger Ralph Kiner won or shared the league home run title for a record seven straight seasons from 1946 to 1952. First baseman Dale Long set a mark in '56 by homering in eight straight games. And pitcher Harvey Haddix made history on May 26, 1959, by pitching 12 perfect innings against the Milwaukee Braves. Unfortunately for Haddix and the Pirates, the no-hitter and the game were lost in the 13th inning.

In 1960, though, Haddix and his teammates capped a tremendous season with an unforgettable World Series performance. Pittsburgh again faced a Yankees team rich with stars such as Mickey Mantle, Roger Maris, Yogi Berra, and Whitey Ford. In the first three games, Pittsburgh was humbled by a combined score of 38–3. But the Pirates won three close games, leading up to Game 7 at Pittsburgh's

Willie Stargell was a fearsome slugger who led Pittsburgh to its last World Series title in 1979.

The right-field wall in the Pirates' sparkling new home, PNC Park, was built 21 feet (6 meters) tall in honor of outfielder Roberto Clemente, whose number 21 was retired in 1973.

On July 12, 1997, Pirates pitchers Francisco Cordova and Ricardo Rincon recorded the only combined extra-inning no-hitter. The Pirates beat the Astros 3–0 in 10 innings.

Forbes Field. There, Bill Mazeroski ended a seesaw struggle with a leadoff homer in the bottom of the ninth, giving the Pirates a 10–9 victory. The second baseman's blast remains the only **walk-off home run** in a World Series Game 7.

Roberto Clemente hit .310 in the 1960 World Series, and the star right fielder led the Pirates back to the series in 1971, against Baltimore. Clemente was the MVP of that series, hitting .414 as the Pirates prevailed four games to three. The beloved 12-time All-Star finished his career by collecting his 3,000th hit on the last day of the 1972 season. Three months later, he died in a plane crash on his way to help earthquake victims in Nicaragua. Clemente's legacy is the large number of major league players today who come from Latin America.

Leadership of the Pirates passed to first baseman Willie "Pops" Stargell. In his 21 seasons, Stargell racked up more homers (475), RBIs (1,540), and extra-base hits (953) than any other player in Pirates history. In 1979, at 39, he captained the Pirates ship to another World Series title. In the process, he pulled off a very rare triple: He was the NL season co-MVP, the NLCS MVP, and the World Series MVP.

Shortstop Jack Wilson made the NL All-Star squad in 2004.

After failing to reach the postseason at any time during the 1980s, the Pirates returned to power a decade later, winning three straight NL East titles from 1990 to 1992. However, they could not get to the World Series, losing once to the Reds and twice to the Braves. The third loss was the toughest. The Braves scored three runs in the bottom of the ninth to win Game 7 of the 1992 NLCS.

The Pirates have not fared well in the NL Central. The change of divisions in 1994 came after the start of a team-record streak of 12 losing seasons. When PNC Park opened in 2001, at least the fans of Pittsburgh could boast of having one of the most beautiful ballparks in the country.

Perhaps the most popular Pirates player ever, Willie Stargell died April 9, 2001, the day the club opened PNC Park. A statue of Stargell greets fans at the left-field entrance to the park.

CHAPTER SIX

The St. Louis Cardinals

Perhaps the NL's most successful franchise, the St. Louis Cardinals club is also one of its oldest, dating to 1876. Only the New York Yankees (with 26) have won more World Series than the Cards' nine. And the Cardinals' history features some of the greatest names ever to play the game.

In the history of the NL, only four players have won the Triple Crown. Rogers Hornsby, a second baseman, won it twice (1922 and 1925). "The Rajah" is also one of only two NL players to hit over .400 for a season, a feat he managed three times. Hornsby's .424 average in 1924 is the modern-day record for highest average over a season. As a manager and player in 1926, he led the Cards to their first World Series title.

In 1934, the Cards put together a team that was as zany, cocky, and fiery as it was talented. Known as the Gashouse Gang, the team was led by pitching brothers Jay ("Dizzy") and Paul ("Daffy") Dean.

This statue of the popular Stan Musial stands outside Busch Stadium.

The Dean brothers won 49 games in the regular season and two each in the Cards' World Series win over the Tigers.

A pair of great Cardinals—Enos "Country" Slaughter and Stan "The Man" Musial—helped bring the team three world championships in the 1940s. Slaughter scored the winning run in Game 7 of the 1946 World Series from first base on a single in what has become known as his "mad dash."

Musial might well be the best, and most popular, player in Cardinals history. In his 22-year career

Albert "Red" Schoendienst, who first joined St. Louis in 1945, wore a Cardinals uniform as a player, coach, or manager for 45 seasons.

Mark McGwire was an intimidating presence at the plate
who was known for hitting mammoth home runs.

with the Redbirds, the slugger earned seven batting crowns, three MVP awards, and a record 24 All-Star Game selections.

Pitching, not hitting, ruled the game of baseball in the late 1960s. The most dominant pitcher in the game was the Cards' hard-throwing right-hander Bob Gibson. In 1968, he was nearly untouchable. That year, he recorded 22 wins, 28 complete games, 13 shutouts, a 1.12 ERA, and 268 strikeouts. He won both the Cy Young and MVP awards.

Much of the success of the '60s-era Cards teams started with speedy outfielder Lou Brock. From 1965 to 1976, the six-time All-Star averaged 65 steals per season and won eight stolen base titles. Brock set a season record of 118 steals in 1974. (That title has since been broken by Ricky Henderson in 1982.) A dangerous hitter as well, Brock collected 3,023 hits on his way to a .293 career average.

The Cards returned to the World Series three times in the 1980s under Manager Whitey Herzog, winning in 1982 and losing in '85 and '87. All three series were tense, seven-game affairs. Taking advantage of the fast artificial turf at Busch Stadium, Herzog's teams featured speed up and down the lineup.

St. Louis joined the NL twice, in 1876 (for two seasons) and again in 1892. From 1892 to 1898, the franchise was known as the Browns. Then in 1899 it was the Perfectos. In 1900, the name Cardinals stuck.

In his poem "The ABC's of Baseball," humorist Ogden Nash wrote this of Rogers Hornsby: "H is for Hornsby, When pitching to Rog, the pitcher would pitch, then the pitcher would dodge."

During Game 7 of the 1934 World Series, Cardinals star Joe "Ducky" Medwick infuriated Detroit players and fans with a hard slide into the Tigers' third baseman. Angry fans threw fruit, eggs, and vegetables at him until baseball commissioner Kenesaw Landis ejected him from the game to calm things down. The Cards won the game 11–0 to take the series.

The road-running Redbirds showed how effective speed and defense could be. In fact, they won the 1982 World Series despite hitting the fewest home runs in the majors! The heart and soul of those Cardinals teams was shortstop Ozzie Smith. "The Wizard of Oz" won 13 straight Gold Glove Awards. He made the difficult plays look routine and the impossible plays look spectacular. Fans loved Ozzie, and his defensive wizardry earned the Hall of Famer 15 All-Star selections.

In 1998, a different kind of Cardinals player captured the nation's attention. Mark McGwire, a huge, slugging first baseman acquired from Oakland the year before, launched an assault on one of baseball's most famous records. Roger Maris's home run mark of 61 (set in 1961) had seemed out of reach for years. But McGwire and Cubs right fielder Sammy Sosa went after it from the season's opening bell. Finally, on September 8, McGwire connected for number 62 off the Cubs' Steve Trachsel. Maris's record was history. With a homer in the season's final game, McGwire closed with 70, topping Sosa's 66. Only McGwire and San Francisco's Barry Bonds (with a new record 73 in 2002) have ever hit 70 or more homers in a season.

Since being placed into the NL Central in 1994, the Cards have often been a major force in the division. Under Manager Tony LaRussa, the club won the division in 1996, 2000, 2001 (shared with Houston), 2002, and 2004. The return to power was fueled by the arrival of stars Jim Edmonds, Albert Pujols, and Scott Rolen. That trio helped power St. Louis to the World Series in 2004, though the Cards were swept in four games by Boston.

In response to the brilliance of Bob Gibson and other dominant pitchers, the mound was lowered from 15 to 10 inches (38 to 25 centimeters) following the 1968 season. The higher the mound, the more the pitcher has an advantage.

Albert Pujols is one of baseball's brightest stars.

Stat Stuff

TEAM RECORDS (THROUGH 2004)

Team	All-time Record	World Series Titles (Most Recent)	Number of Times in the Postseason	Top Manager (Wins)
Chicago Cubs	9,814–9,271	2 (1908)	14	Cap Anson (1,283)
Cincinnati	9,447–9,115	5 (1990)	12	Sparky Anderson (863)
Houston	3,408–3,430	0	8	Bill Virdon (544)
Milwaukee*	2,679–3,019	0	2	Phil Garner (585)
Pittsburgh	9,422–9,101	5 (1979)	14	Fred Clarke (1,422)
St. Louis	9,583–8,972	9 (1982)	20	Red Schoendienst (1,041)

*includes Seattle

NATIONAL LEAGUE CENTRAL
CAREER LEADERS (THROUGH 2004)
Chicago

Category	Name (Years with Team)	Total
Batting Average	Bill Madlock (1974–76)	.336
Home Runs	Sammy Sosa (1992–2004)	545
RBI	Cap Anson (1876–1897)	1,879
Stolen Bases	Frank Chance (1898–1912)	400
Wins	Charlie Root (1926–1941)	201
Saves	Lee Smith (1980–87)	180
Strikeouts	Ferguson Jenkins (1966–1973, 1982–83)	2,038

NATIONAL LEAGUE CENTRAL CAREER LEADERS (THROUGH 2004)

Cincinnati

Category	Name (Years with Team)	Total
Batting Average	Cy Seymour (1902–06)	.332
Home Runs	Johnny Bench (1967–1983)	389
RBI	Johnny Bench (1967–1983)	1,376
Stolen Bases	Bid McPhee (1882–1899)	568
Wins	Eppa Rixey (1921–1933)	179
Saves	Danny Graves (1997–2004)	172
Strikeouts	Jim Maloney (1960–1970)	1,592

Houston

Category	Name (Years with Team)	Total
Batting Average	Lance Berkman (1999–2004)	.303
Home Runs	Jeff Bagwell (1991–2004)	446
RBI	Jeff Bagwell (1991–2004)	1,510
Stolen Bases	Cesar Cedeno (1970–1981)	487
Wins	Joe Niekro (1975–1985)	144
Saves	Billy Wagner (1995–present)	225
Strikeouts	Nolan Ryan (1980–88)	1,866

Milwaukee

Category	Name (Years with Team)	Total
Batting Average	Jeff Cirillo (1994–99)	.307
Home Runs	Robin Yount (1974–1993)	251
RBI	Robin Yount (1974–1993)	1,406
Stolen Bases	Paul Molitor (1978–1992)	412
Wins	Jim Slaton (1971–77, 1979–1983)	117
Saves	Dan Plesac (1986–1992)	133
Strikeouts	Teddy Higuera (1985–1994)	1,081

NATIONAL LEAGUE CENTRAL CAREER LEADERS (THROUGH 2004)

Pittsburgh

Category	Name (Years with Team)	Total
Batting Average	Paul Waner (1926–1940)	.340
Home Runs	Willie Stargell (1962–1982)	475
RBI	Willie Stargell (1962–1982)	1,540
Stolen Bases	Max Carey (1910–1926)	688
Wins	Wilbur Cooper (1912–1924)	202
Saves	Roy Face (1953–1968)	188
Strikeouts	Bob Friend (1951–1965)	1,682

St. Louis

Category	Name (Years with Team)	Total
Batting Average	Rogers Hornsby (1915–1926, 1933)	.359
Home Runs	Stan Musial (1941–1963)	475
RBI	Stan Musial (1941–1963)	1,951
Stolen Bases	Lou Brock (1964–1979)	888
Wins	Bob Gibson (1959–1975)	251
Saves	Lee Smith (1990–93)	160
Strikeouts	Bob Gibson (1959–1975)	3,117

Glossary

ace—the best pitcher on a baseball team

Cy Young Award—the award annually given to the best pitcher in the league

dynasty—a team that wins a number of championships in a short period of time

free agent—a player who has completed his contract with one team and is free to sign with any other team

no-hitters—complete games in which the pitcher or pitchers for one team do not allow the opposing team any hits

pennant—the championship of each league (American and National)

postseason—the playoffs, which start with the Division Series, continue with the League Championship Series, and conclude with the World Series

professional—describes someone who receives pay for his or her services or activities—in this case, playing baseball as a livelihood

saves—the measure of a late-inning relief pitcher with his team in the lead who finishes the game with his team winning the game

tradition—elements passed down from generation to generation (or from team to team)

Triple Crown—for a hitter, it means leading the league in batting average, home runs, and RBIs in the same season; less often, it refers to a pitcher who leads the league in wins, strikeouts, and ERAs in the same season

underdog—a team that is not expected to win

walk-off home run—a home run that ends the game (in this case, it ended the World Series)

wild card—a team that finishes in second place in its division but still makes the playoffs

World Series—baseball's championship event; the winners of the AL and the NL pennants annually meet in a best-of-seven series to determine the world champion

Time Line

1869 The Cincinnati Red Stockings are baseball's first all-professional team.

1876 The NL begins play, with Chicago, Cincinnati, and St. Louis among the charter franchises.

1882 The Pittsburgh Alleghenys are formed; they become known as the Pirates in 1891.

1908 The Cubs win the World Series for the second consecutive year.

1924 St. Louis second baseman Rogers Hornsby bats .424, still a big-league record.

1926 The Cardinals win the first of their NL-best nine World Series titles.

1962 The Houston Colt .45s join the NL as an expansion team (a new franchise); they become known as the Astros in 1965.

1969 The Seattle Pilots debut in the AL West; one year later, they move to Milwaukee and become the Brewers.

1975 The Cincinnati Reds win the first of back-to-back World Series.

1979 First baseman Willie Stargell leads the Pirates to their fifth World Series championship.

1980 The Astros win a division title and make the playoffs for the first time.

1982 The Brewers win their first and, so far, only pennant in club history; they lose in the World Series.

1998 The Brewers move from the AL to the NL.

Cardinals first baseman Mark McGwire blasts 70 home runs to break Roger Maris's single-season record; McGwire outduels Chicago's Sammy Sosa, who finishes with 66 homers.

For More Information

BOOKS

Christopher, Matt. *At the Plate with Sammy Sosa*. Boston: Little Brown & Co., 1999.

Doherty, Craig A., and Katherine M. Doherty. *The Houston Astrodome*. Woodbridge, Conn.: Blackbirch Press, 1997.

Rambeck, Richard. *Milwaukee Brewers: AL East*. Mankato, Minn.: Creative Education, 1992.

Stewart, Mark. *Mark McGwire: Home Run King*. New York: Children's Press, 1999.

ON THE WEB

Visit our home page for lots of links about the National League Central teams: *http://www.childsworld.com/links.html*

Note to Parents, Teachers, and Librarians: We routinely check our Web links to make sure they're safe, active sites—so encourage your readers to check them out!

Index

ABOUT THE AUTHOR

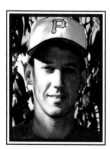

John Silbaugh is a middle-school teacher in Colorado, where he lives with his wife and three daughters. A lifelong fan of the Pirates, John has worked as a tour guide at Coors Field, the home park of the Colorado Rockies. This is his first book.